Christmas Quickies Cookbook
© Mel Alafaci 2023

First printed November 2023 by Ingram Spark

All rights reserved. Except as permitted under the Australian Copyright Act 1968 (for example, a fair dealing for the purposes of study, research, criticism or review), no part of this book may be reproduced, stored in a retrieval system, communicated or transmitted in any form or by any means without prior written permission.

Creator: Mel Alafaci (Author)
Title: Christmas Quickies Cookbook
ISBN: 9780645808483 (Paperback)
Subjects: Cook Book

Typesetting by Chloe Reynolds - Social Chloe

Chef Mel is taking on the WORLD!

With a smile that can light up a room, Chef Mel Alafaci has become a globally recognised chef and food educator. Her recent success in the USA means she's Australia's hottest rising culinary personality. Born in Zimbabwe, Chef Mel lived in South Africa before moving to Australia and starting her reign in the global foodie market.

She has an unwavering passion for cooking, eating, and teaching. And her intoxicating enthusiasm, authenticity, and unique culinary lingo will have you hungry to flex your muscles in the kitchen. Chef Mel is brilliant at adding humour, shortcuts, tricks, and hacks to all those tedious tasks, as well as making the scary ones simple and easy to accomplish.

CHEF MEL THE HAPPY CHEF | @CHEFMEL_HAPPYCHEF | WWW.CHEFMEL.ME

ABOUT MEL

Mel Alafaci has been passionate about food her whole life. She's the founder of Vanilla Zulu Cooking School, one of Australia's leading cooking schools, and has more than 28 years of professional cooking experience.

People battle to say her surname... so to make it easy she calls herself CHEF MEL.

WILD ABOUT FOOD!

Recipes

Recipes

Breads & Feasting Table Ideas

- 3 — Santa's Favorite Loaf
- 5 — Whipped Festive Butters
- 6 — Fragrant Festive Crackers

Starters & Side Dishes

- 9 — Paté with Burnt Sage Butter
- 11 — Turkey & Porcini Tart with Parsnip Tangle Fries
- 12 — Festive Feasting Table with Prosciutto High Heel
- 14 — Festive Butternut & Saffron Broth
- 15 — Pear & Parma Carpaccio
- 16 — Oysters Rockefeller

Salads & Stacks

- 18 — Kipfler Potato Salad
- 19 — Christmassy Caprese Salad
- 20 — Personalised Festive Salads in a Jar
- 21 — Christmassy Ceviche Stacks

Recipes

Meat, Fish & Mains

24	Tremendously Tender Moist Turkey
27	Sexy Roast Vegetables
29	Marmalade or Maple Vanilla Spiced Glazed Ham
30	Ginger & Lemon Baked Salmon
31	Festive Stuffed Pumpkin

Sweet Treats

34	Vanilla Berry Bombe Alaska
36	Boozy Panna Cotta
38	Pistachio Lemon Butter Cookies
39	Ice Cream with Pistachio Black Salt Praline
40	Peppermint Bark
41	Christmas Hot Chocolates
43	Gingerbread Cookies
45	Sticky Date & Brandy Pudding
46	Christmas Trifle Cups

THE LITTLE BOOK OF *Christmas Leftovers* Recipes

52	Glamorous Turkey & Cream Cheese Balls
53	Crispy Spring Rolls
54	Croquettes
55	Stuffed Chicken
56	Party Pies
58	The Ultimate Leftover Stacks
59	Quesadillas
60	Chef's Salad with Mel's Secret Dressing
62	Happy Sexy Quickie Eggs
63	Tea Cup Quiche

Breads & Feasting Table Ideas

Delicious morsels to share and celebrate with.

Santa's Favourite Loaf

Santa's Favourite Loaf

SERVINGS: 2-4

INGREDIENTS

DOUGH
- 450g plain or baker's flour
- 2 teaspoons instant yeast
- 2 teaspoons sugar
- 320ml lukewarm water
- 1 teaspoon salt
- 30ml oil
- 2 teaspoons extra flour
- 2 tablespoons polenta
- Cooking spray to grease the baking tray

TOPPINGS
- 1/2 teaspoon sexy black salt flakes *or good-quality flake salt*
- 1 tablespoon finely chopped rosemary gravel
- 3 large lashings of extra virgin olive oil

CHRISTMAS TREE GARNISH
- 12 olives
- 12 cherry tomatoes

METHOD

Add the yeast to the warm water, with the 2 teaspoons of extra flour and sugar, stir and set aside for about 10 minutes until foamy.

Once foamy, mix this liquid with the flour, salt, and oil until it forms a smooth dough. Place on a floured surface and knead until the dough is smooth and pliable. Use your mixer and a dough hook if you are not doing this by hand, about 5-7 minutes at least.

Place the dough into a greased bowl and cover it with a clean wet cloth, and allow to prove for about 15 minutes or until doubled in size. Grease a baking tray with the cooking spray and then add the polenta, and shake to coat the tray. Remove the dough ball from the covered bowl and place it on the polenta baking tray.

Make deep holes (Nona's fingerprints) using your fingertips to poke the dough. If you are making this into a Christmas tree shape, simply press and pinch it into shape.

Garnish with the sexy black salt flakes, rosemary gravel, and oil. Then add olives and cherry tomatoes. Allow to prove on the bench for 20-30 minutes until doubled in size or pop in the fridge for up to 4 hours to delay the cooking time if you prefer.

Bake at 200°C for about 12-15 minutes until brown and cooked through.

Serve with extra virgin olive oil and balsamic vinegar.

Whipped truffle butter

Whipped Festive Butters

SERVINGS: 8-12

INGREDIENTS

LEMON AND HERB WHIPPED BUTTER
250g salted butter
2 teaspoons fresh herbs like rosemary, thyme or oregano
2 teaspoons chopped parsley
1 teaspoon lemon zest
1 teaspoon crushed or freshly ground black pepper

WHIPPED TRUFFLE BUTTER
250g salted butter
1 tablespoon truffle paste, truffle tapenade or fresh truffles

WHIPPED STINKY BUTTER
(LIKE SEXY GARLIC BUTTER...My personal favourite)
250g salted butter
2 teaspoons fresh herbs like rosemary, thyme or oregano
2 teaspoons chopped parsley
1 teaspoon crushed garlic
2 tablespoons minced or chopped olives
1 small chilli finely chopped - Optional

METHOD

Whipped butters are amazing to serve with your fresh Santa's loaf. You can also use this idea at dinner parties and family meals during the rest of the year.

You can choose hundreds of different flavours for your whipped butter, the method will always remain the same.

First, grate the butter. When you grate cold butter it is INSTANTLY soft. Place it in your stand mixer with a whisk attachment. Do not try to do this by hand it's just too much hard work)

Beat on a medium speed for about 8 minutes, then scrape the sides of the bowl, and then whip at a higher speed for another 6 minutes, or until the butter has turned from yellow to a pale light colour...almost white. Now add YOUR selection of flavours and mix through.

Decant into a festive bowl, or place into an airtight container or greaseproof paper (and then roll like a bonbon or cracker and twist the edges to seal. Store in the fridge until ready to serve. If you have stored this in greaseproof paper, use a hot knife to cut off roundels of the whipped butter and store the rest!

Fragrant Festive Crackers

SERVINGS: 6-8

INGREDIENTS

CRACKERS
- 1 cup plain flour
- 80ml water
- 20 ml melted butter OR olive oil
- 1 teaspoon chopped herbs like rosemary, thyme, oregano
- 1 teaspoon seeds like sesame, nigella, poppy
- 1/2 teaspoon crushed black peppercorns
- pinch salt

TOPPINGS

You could add a combination and keep changing these depending on what you are serving them with.
They are so much fun!
- 1 teaspoon lemon zest
- 1 teaspoon dill
- 1 teaspoon chilli flakes for a crab or prawn dip or pate
- You could use rose petals and black salt.

Try these YOUR way. They are even good plain.

METHOD

Simply place the flour, bling, spices, and liquid together in a bowl and mix with a spoon to form a dough ball. Now dust your hands and surface with flour to prevent the dough from being annoying and sticking to everything. Knead the dough for about 3 minutes until the dough is nice and soft and pliable.

Take a teaspoonful of dough and roll it out into long, thin biscuits, or roll all the dough out and use a cookie cutter to cut shapes, making sure you use lots of flour underneath so they don't stick to the counter. Make sure your dough is as thin as possible. Bake hot and fast on an ungreased baking tray for about 3-8 minutes at 200°C. They should be brittle and not too brown! Store them in an airtight container until you want to use them.

Starters & Side Dishes

The perfect way to start the celebrations.

Pâté with Burnt Sage Butter

Pâté with Burnt Sage Butter

SERVINGS: 6-8

INGREDIENTS

500 g chicken livers *OR 2 cups mushrooms* finely diced
80 g bacon, diced
1 large onion, finely sliced
1 clove garlic, optional
1 teaspoon chopped thyme or sage
80 g butter
80 ml cream
80 ml chicken stock
30 ml brandy

BURNT SAGE BUTTER TOPPING
80g butter
1 teaspoon chopped sage leaves

METHOD

Trim the chicken livers if necessary. Rinse and pat dry.
Melt the butter in a frying pan and then when hot fry the bacon until brown and crisp.
Add the onions and the garlic and allow to cook through. Now add livers OR the mushrooms.

Cook livers till slightly pink inside; do not overcook them as they will be grainy.

Cook the mushrooms until beautifully soft. Add the thyme and liquids leaving the cream for last. Season to taste and then allow to cool once chicken livers or mushrooms have cooked through.
Place in blender and blend until smooth.
Place in ramekin dishes or other suitable dishes and top with extra virgin olive oil or melted butter if you are not serving the pate immediately.
Serve with melba toast or fresh bread. Delicious.

BURNT SAGE BUTTER
Heat the butter and the leaves over high heat until the butter melts and the foam rises to the top.
When the foam heats it will go nice and small and eventually a nutty brown.
Remove from heat and pour over the plate. Allow to set in the fridge and serve.

Turkey & Porcini Tart with Parsnip Tangle Fries

Turkey & Porcini Tart with Parsnip Tangle Fries

SERVINGS: 8-12

INGREDIENTS

PASTRY
125g butter
200g flour
Pinch salt
125g cream cheese, mascarpone or crème fraîche

PARSNIP CHIPS
1 parsnip, peeled
vegetable oil for frying

FILLING
30ml olive oil
1 large white onion finely chopped
450g turkey breast finely shaved or diced
10ml porcini dust (blend down dehydrated mushroom)
5ml flake salt *or use chicken stock powder*
60g cream cheese
120ml cream
40g soft butter

METHOD

PASTRY

Mix the butter and cream cheese through the flour till it resembles bread crumbs then knead the dough together.

Grate the butter into the flour and then pinch in till the flour resembles breadcrumbs and the butter is evenly distributed. Add the salt and the cream cheese and mix through, or use a food processor to combine. Do not overwork the dough! Roll into a dough ball and then cover and chill for about an hour before rolling out.

FILLING

Heat the oil in a frying pan and add the onions, stir until cooked for about 3-5 minutes, and then add the turkey sliced or diced, the porcini powder, and seasoning. Once the turkey has cooked then add the cream, adjust the seasoning, add the butter and blend to a thick paste in a food processor or blender.

You can change the flavour of this paste as often as you like:

Add fresh lemon zest and thyme and black pepper

Add fresh lime zest and chilli and coriander

Add fresh sage and pink peppercorns

Add saffron and lemon zest

Be as creative as you like!

PARSNIP CHIPS

Simply cut down a peeled parsnip with the Asian Julienne grater and fry in vegetable oil until crispy. I also do this in my air fryer which is much easier. Just pop in the air fryer once you have drizzled the ribbons with a bit of oil...then cook for about 4-5 minutes until brown and crispy.

I have used pastry bases using the cream cheese pastry recipes to make it into a gorgeous tart! Bake the tart shells as per the recipe, fill with the turkey paste, garnish with the parsnip tangle fries and then season with bling and serve!

Festive Feasting Table with Prosciutto High Heel

SERVINGS: 4-6

INGREDIENTS

16-20 slices of prosciutto/parma ham cut to 1mm thickness at your deli
1 medium terracotta pot or similar vessel
Figs or herbs or edible flowers to garnish

METHOD

Turn the terracotta pot upside down and then start draping the prosciutto or parma ham over the pot with the fat side presenting on the outside.
Continue to drape until you have covered the bowl, I usually allow 2-3 slices per person depending on what this is being served with.
Garnish with cut figs, petals, or sprigs of fresh herbs.
You can do this the day before and then wrap it with cling film or plastic wrap.
It's perfect for cheese boards, and feasting platters and is highly mobile and so very glamorous!

Festive Butternut & Saffron Broth

Festive Butternut & Saffron Broth

SERVINGS: 6-8

INGREDIENTS

2 teaspoons butter or olive oil
2 medium onions chopped
2 cloves garlic, crushed
2 good pinches of saffron or use 1 teaspoon of turmeric powder instead
600g -1 kg butternut, sweet potato, or pumpkin cubed into 1 or 2 cm cubes (perfect way to use leftovers)
2 litres of good chicken or vegetable stock
Salt and pepper to season
Zest one lime
1 small chilli crushed (or use more if you like!)
2 tablespoons Parmesan cheese or use mature cheddar (optional)
80 – 100 ml fresh cream
100 g Danish-style feta mixed to a paste with 1 bunch of chives or spring onions, finely chopped.
Alternatively, use Greek feta blended with a few tablespoons of cream until smooth.
1 tablespoon fried shallots (optional)

METHOD

Fry the onions in the oil or butter with the garlic until just soft.

Now add the saffron or turmeric and finely cubed butternut and the stock.

Allow to come to a boil and cook for about 15 -25 minutes until the butternut is soft.

Now add the zest, chilli, and cheese (optional) as well as the fresh cream.

Remove from heat and blend with a stick blender, and blend until ridiculously velvety and smooth.
If this is too thick for your liking add some more stock and thin it down.

When you serve simply garnish with dollops of feta and chives and even some fried shallots for crunch!

Pear & Parma Carpaccio

SERVINGS: 4-6

INGREDIENTS

2-3 pears/apples/quince sliced thickly and roasted
2-3 sliced prosciutto or parma per person
1 tablespoon goats cheese/cream cheese, per person
edible flowers and herb fronds
chives chopped up and placed in a bowl

DRESSING
20ml honey
80ml verjuice
50ml olive oil
(all mixed together)
salt, and pepper to taste

METHOD

Place the sliced pears/apples/quince on a greased baking tray and then bake at 225-250°C for about 20-25 minutes until dried and crisp! Place one slice of parma ham/prosciutto onto a plate.
Mix the goat's cheese in a bowl until nice and smooth.
Roll 1 tablespoon of the cheese into a ball and then roll through the chopped-up herbs and petals. And top onto your baked fruit slice.
Serve with micro herbs, rocket, and some of the dressing.

Oysters Rockefeller

SERVINGS: 4-6

INGREDIENTS

2 dozen fresh, shucked oysters
1 cup freshly chopped baby spinach
1/2 cup shallots finely chopped
4 tablespoons grated Parmesan or Cheddar
1 cup fresh breadcrumbs
3 rashers streaky bacon, diced
80 g butter, melted
2 tablespoons parsley, chopped

METHOD

Mix all of your ingredients into a large bowl. Mix to combine.
Top fresh oysters with a mixture of spinach, shallots, bacon, breadcrumbs, Parmesan cheese, and the butter.
Bake in an oven of 200c for about 8-12 minutes until bubbly and golden.

Salads & Stacks

Sublime sides to adorn the table.

Kipfler Potato Salad

SERVINGS: 6-8

INGREDIENTS

1 kg Kipfler Potato or use baby potatoes (or just any potato!) scrubbed and boiled
1 small onion finely sliced
100 g bacon or chorizo or speck or prosciutto diced
250g tub sour cream or crème fraiche
3 tablespoons chopped chives or parsley
Salt and pepper to season

METHOD

Slice the potatoes (or leave them whole if they are small).
Fry the bacon bits in a hot pan until nice and brown and crispy, add the finely chopped onion, reduce the heat and then stir until the onion is soft. Remove pan from heat.

Now add the potatoes into the bacon onion mix in the pan and then add the sour cream/crème fraiche, chives, or parsley and then stir to coat. Season to taste and then serve!

I garnish it with edible petals and micro herbs to make this salad look ten times more expensive!

Christmassy Caprese Salad

SERVINGS: 4-6

INGREDIENTS

2-3 ripe truss or Roma tomatoes, thickly sliced
Lots of fresh basil leaves
6-8 slices fior de latte, bocconcini balls or mozzarella slices
Salt and pepper to season
Balsamic vinegar to drizzle
Extra virgin olive oil to drizzle

METHOD

This is a beautiful festive salad.
It can be made days in advance and stored.
Serve with the fresh basil leaves as you plate it.
You can simply arrange the ripe tomato slices with the deliciously creamy cheese in the shape of a candy cane.

Personalised Festive Salads in a Jar

SERVINGS: 4-6

INGREDIENTS

2-3 ripe truss or Roma tomatoes or cherry tomatoes, thickly sliced or halved
Lots of fresh basil leaves, lettuce leaves or rocket
6-8 slices fior de latte, bocconcini balls or mozzarella slices
1-2 cups Assorted chopped veggies of your choice like corn, beans, carrots, lettuce
1 cup chicken mayo, crab mayo, turkey mayo or lobster mayo
(just mix shredded meat of your choice and bind lightly with mayo)

METHOD

This is a beautiful festive salad that can be made in individual jars in case you have to travel or take a starter to your festive event. The possibilities are endless, so be creative.
Use lots of red, green and white ingredients and remember to take the dressing separately.
You can then use a Christmas Tag to make everyone feel extremely special with their own personal jar.
You can even wrap them with festive paper and a ribbon as a gift.
They can be made days in advance and stored.
Keep chilled if you are travelling with these; they are extremely easy to move around and serve!

Christmassy Ceviche Stacks

SERVINGS: 4-6

INGREDIENTS

400g Diced fresh fish, prawns or shrimp
50-80ml lemon or lime juice, freshly squeezed
1 red or pink onion finely chopped
Salt and pepper to season
½ cup finely chopped coriander/cilantro or your favourite herb
1 red capsicum/pepper chopped
1/2 cup halved cherry tomatoes
2 tablespoons olive oil

METHOD

Perfect made the day before, or at least 4 hours before serving.
Place diced fish or seafood in a large bowl.
Dress with the lemon or lime juice, salt and pepper.
Cover and then place in the fridge for at least 4 hours, or overnight.
Stir and check the seasoning. You can now add the freshly chopped onion, herbs and vegetables.
Serve in individual glasses or bowls, or use a stacking ring to create a festive stack on the plate.
Serve cold with crostini toast or salad leaves.

Meat, Fish & Mains

The hero of the festive table.

Tremendously Tender Moist Turkey

Tremendously Tender Moist Turkey

SERVINGS: 8-12

INGREDIENTS

TURKEY
1 turkey between 3 and 5 kilograms

STUFFING
200g streaky bacon finely chopped
400g pork minced and finely chopped or use pork sausage meat
2 cups onion finely chopped
1 cup fresh breadcrumbs/roast sweet potato /roast potato
2 tablespoons freshly chopped sage
2 cloves garlic (optional)
Zest and juice of one lemon (optional)
1 teaspoon turmeric (purely for colour)
3 tablespoons naughty butter
(this will help give the turkey breast personality and flavour)
Pinch salt
Pinch nutmeg

METHOD

Preheat your oven to 190°C to 200°C. Heat a frying pan or large enough pan with a little canola spray or vegetable oil. Add the bacon to the pan when the pan is sworn word hot - it should sizzle and 'talk' to you. Don't stir straight away, let the first lot of bacon on the bottom brown deliciously before stirring. Lots of stirring will cool down the pan too quickly and you don't want bacon stew. If you are worried, at any stage, about this burning give the pan a good firm 'cheffy' shake.

Once the bacon is sexy and brown and the fat has rendered out the bacon, keep the heat high and add the pork mince. Let the pan return to temperature and only stir to prevent it from burning. Using two forks to get rid of the pork mince lumps is a good idea, I also sometimes stab my mince with the base of a whisk…breaks it up well!

When the pork components are brown and beautiful you can now add the finely diced onions, garlic, sage, lemon zest, turmeric, and nutmeg. Reduce the heat and allow those onions to cook down. I know this seems like a lot of onion, but you will thank me! When soft and it all smells like a little bit of heaven, add the butter, breadcrumbs/roast sweet potato or cooked potato, and lemon juice. Stir and season. Allow to cool.

Now, while the stuffing is cooling, you can tackle the turkey. What we are going to do here is cut the turkey down the backbone and then open it out flat so that it cooks faster. We can get a 3.5kg bird to cook down in 1.5 hours by using this technique. You need a big board and a sharp knife. Place the turkey breast down on the board. Cut down the backbone either to the left or right of the spine (don't cut directly in the middle it's just too difficult!). Once the back is open turn the bird over and break its breastbone with your palm and break it flat. Place on the roasting tray. Put the neck side facing closest to you and then loosen the skin away from the turkey down to the drumsticks, you're creating a 'turkey envelope' to put your stuffing into!

Use a large tablespoon to feed the cool stuffing onto each breast and then push the stuffing down right over the drumstick. Refill on top of the breast and then reshape the bird.

Rub the skin with lots of olive oil and salt. I even add a bit of turmeric, just a sprinkle, to the skin and rub some oil in with it to create a turkey spray tan. Season with salt and then place in the oven for approximately 1 hour and 45 minutes. Check if juices are running clear, I always check in the breast down by the breastbone to make sure. All that juicy goodness will cook into the usually boring turkey meat and this turkey will be terrific to carve too. Delicious!

EXTRA STUFFING

If you have stuffing left over, take a piece of foil, grease it well and then roll the remaining stuffing into a sausage. Seal the foil and bake for about half an hour before serving the bird.

Sexy Roast Vegetables
(not the pale soggy ones!)

SERVINGS: 2-4

INGREDIENTS

1 cup diced sweet potato
1 cup diced cauliflower
1 cup diced carrot
1 cup diced beetroot
1 cup diced potato
1 cup diced pumpkin

METHOD

CHEF'S NOTE

Always go for colour! Some veggies are better for roasting and some are better for steaming. These veggies are BETTER roasted swear word hot and fast at 220C...this amount of veggies in an oven of 180C will throw SO much steam that they will NEVER go brown.

So, crank the oven up to swear word hot so that we get LOTS of colour in these veggies. When vegetables are roasted they caramelise and give 100% more flavour and personality than when steamed.
I do about a 3cm dice, but you can go bigger or smaller. The larger they are the longer they will take to cook.

Place on a tray and then drizzle with extra virgin olive oil, your choice of spices, salt and pepper. Not too much, these don't need to be drowned or over-spiced, they will be sexy just with a little love.
Cook in a SWEAR WORD HOT oven (220C) for 35 minutes, less if your dice is smaller.
You can use any combination of vegetables that you have available to you.

I always add some green veg after I've roasted the sexy veggies to add some colour and texture.
I steam either beans, snow peas, broccoli or asparagus and then add to the mix.
You can then serve these with a main course, or on their own with either a pea puree or chickpea/butter bean mash to hold the stack together.

Marmalade or Maple Vanilla Spiced Glazed Ham

Marmalade or Maple Vanilla Spiced Glazed Ham

SERVINGS: 8-12

INGREDIENTS

3kg Ham joint from butcher or supermarket, bone in or out
1 jar marmalade or 250ml maple syrup
20ml Vanilla Bean Paste
15-25 cloves, whole
Pinch nutmeg
1 teaspoon turmeric powder

METHOD

This is a real quickie and is very lazy indeed.
You can do this glazing the day before and bake the ham on the day, or you can bake the day back and serve this cold and ready-to-slice.
I have sprinkled mine with black salt and rose petals to serve, and have removed the cloves, but it will look gorgeous just as it is with that sexy golden crust.
I have used marmalade for my glaze, but feel free to use maple syrup.
Preheat the oven to 200°C. Mix the marmalade OR maple syrup, vanilla, nutmeg, and turmeric together in a bowl until it forms a thick smooth paste.

Take the skin off the ham, leaving a skinny layer of fat behind.
You can score the fat with your sharp knife, making diamond shapes or squares in the fat.
Place the ham into a suitable baking dish, and then start to rub or brush it onto the surface of the ham, making sure you cover everything evenly. If you have any left, keep this for basting later in the cooking process.

You can now stud this ham with the cloves, making patterns on the crisscross of the lines you made with the knife into the fat, or just stud evenly.
Bake the ham in the hot oven, for 40-50 minutes, then baste if you need to with the remaining glaze.
You want to ensure the marmalade or maple glaze has turned into a delightful golden crust.
You can turn the heat down after 50 minutes and hold it at 75OC if you are not ready to serve.
You can now carve this and serve or allow it to cool and carve and serve when cold.

Maple, Ginger & Lemon Baked Salmon

SERVINGS: 8-10

INGREDIENTS

1 side of salmon, approx. 1.5-2 kg
2 lemons, zested and then juiced
1 tablespoon grated ginger
1 teaspoon crushed garlic
50 ml melted butter or veggie oil
1 teaspoon chilli flakes, optional
50 ml honey or maple
Salt and pepper to season well

METHOD

Place the salmon into a large baking dish.
Mix the lemon juice, lemon zest, ginger, garlic and chilli with the butter/oil and maple/honey together.
Baste the salmon with this delicious mix, leaving any remaining liquid for glazing later.
Bake hot and fast at 220C for approximately 45 minutes to an hour, until the fish is cooked through and golden brown and sticky. You can baste with some more of the remaining liquid at about the half an hour mark.
Check if the fish is cooked with a knife or fork if it flakes easily it is cooked.
You can serve salmon still pink in the middle, but it depends on your personal choice.

Festive Stuffed Pumpkin

SERVINGS: 6-8 AS MAINS

INGREDIENTS

1 small pumpkin
2 tins cannellini or butter bean or chickpeas
2 cups fresh breadcrumbs or cauliflower 'rice'
2 tablespoons ras el hanout/ curry powder or smoked paprika or your choice of spice
1 cup melted butter or olive oil or alternative to bind or use cream cheese if you prefer (make this your way)
1 pack of minced vegetable sausage, optional
100g feta, cheddar, or goats cheese or cheese alternative
Salt and pepper to season
1 tablespoon porcini mushroom powder OR 1/2 cup fresh mushrooms chopped

METHOD

Cut the lid of the pumpkin off and remove the seeds with a strong spoon. Place on a plate and microwave for 8-12 until pre-cooked and tender. Mix the stuffing ingredients together in a bowl and season to taste. Spoon the stuffing into the pre-cooked pumpkin and pack it down. Season and moisturise the pumpkin skin with some more olive oil, salt, and pepper, and then bake in a small frying pan or dish for 35 minutes, until the stuffing and the pumpkin skin are delicious and golden.
Perfect to serve to the table, cut into slices and serve.

Sweet Treats

Show them you love them with these sweet treats!

Vanilla Berry Bombe Alaska

Vanilla Berry Bombe Alaska

SERVINGS: 6-8
MAKE INTO INDIVIDUAL SERVINGS, OR ONE LARGE BOMBE

INGREDIENTS

4 egg whites, room temperature
1/2 teaspoon cream of tartar
Juice of one lemon, about 30ml
5ml Vanilla Bean paste
1 cup sugar
1/2 cup water
1 cup frozen berries of your choice, puréed in a food processor until smooth
2 litres best vanilla bean ice cream, softened
1 cup chopped cookies, *cookie dough, muffin, Christmas mince pie, panettone, Madeira cake, meringues OR honeycomb OR brownie. You get to choose!*
60 ml brandy to flambe

METHOD

Take 4-6 teacups and pack with a layer of the softened ice cream, then the berry layer, then the cookies or brownie, etc, top again with the ice cream layer, and return to the freezer. You can do this for individual servings, or use a large bowl to create a single, larger bombe.

Place the sugar and the water in a large frying pan and stir to dissolve the sugar into the water, brush any sugar on the side of the frying pan down with a wet pastry brush. Feel free to do this over very high heat, we want the sugar to reach 120°C.

Before your sugar gets to temp, you have time to whip the egg whites, cream of tartar, lemon juice and vanilla bean paste until stiff peaks form, preferably in a strong stand mixer.
Once the sugar syrup is at 120°C, add it to the egg white mix at a very high speed so that it incorporates. Whip until shiny and gorgeous.
Un-mould the ice cream from the cups, smother it with this beautiful meringue, and then hit it with a blowtorch until the meringue is gorgeous and brown.

Heat the brandy in a small saucepan. Once hot and bubbling light safely from the side of the rim of the pan with a long match or safety lighter, and ensure you avert your face. Shake the brandy to keep it alight, and then pour over the Bombe and serve.
Eat and enjoy. This recipe can be made in advance and then frozen.

Practise this a few times if you want, just to ensure you can do this in front of your guests!

Boozy Panna Cotta

SERVINGS: 4-6

INGREDIENTS

400ml fresh cream
60g white sugar or use honey or maple or sweetener
100ml Amarula or Baileys or just use milk
2 sheets of gold-strength leaf gelatine or two teaspoons of powdered gelatine
5 ml vanilla paste or extract
pinch nutmeg
pinch cinnamon
4-6 star anise

TOPPING

2-3 Christmas Mince pies chopped into small pieces to decorate or use chocolate curls, broken biscuits etc.

METHOD

Get your glass jars ready, we will pour the hot liquid directly into these. You will need about 4, but feel free to double or triple this recipe as you need. Wine glasses or bowls are also perfect for panna cotta.

Heat the cream, milk, vanilla, spices and sugar to a boil. Remove from heat and allow to cool slightly. Stir through the Amarula/Baileys/milk.
Soak the gelatine in cold water for a few minutes until very soft. Remove the gelatine leaves from the water and then stir into the warm cream. You can pour the liquid into the ramekins.
Allow to cool to room temperature then refrigerate until ready to serve. You can store these, sealed, for up to four days!

TO SERVE

Decorate with chopped Christmas Mince pies.
You could also use honeycomb, toffee, sliced fruit, or a scoop of ice cream!

Pistachio Lemon Butter Cookies

Pistachio Lemon Butter Cookies

SERVINGS: 6-12

INGREDIENTS

COOKIES

1 cup or 225g butter
1 cup or 220g white sugar
1 teaspoon vanilla
Zest one small lemon
1 egg
3 cups or 450 g plain flour
1 teaspoon baking powder
3 tablespoons finely chopped pistachio, or use the nut you prefer
Half a teaspoon of salt, 1/4 teaspoon of nutmeg and 1/4 teaspoon of cinnamon.

ICING

450g (3 cups) icing sugar mixture
hot water to bind...add a drop at a time.
2 drops liquid food colouring

METHOD

YOU WILL NEED 1 set of Star Christmas Tree Cooking Cutters from your kitchen store or online.
Preheat your oven to 180°C.
Cream the butter and sugar together in the stand mixer with the whisk attachment. Mix the rest of the ingredients into the whipped butter and sugar mix until it just forms a lovely firm dough. Cover with a wet cloth and allow to rest in the fridge for about 15 minutes.
Roll these out on a well-floured surface, ensuring they don't stick. Keep moving your dough as you roll it to prevent it from sticking to the surface. Roll to about 5-8mm and use your Christmas star cookie cutters set to get a set of star cookies ranging from large to small to create a tree like in the photo.
I got my cutter set online as a set!

Place on a greased baking sheet and bake at 180oC for about 12-18 minutes, until the cookies are brown and delicious, and then allow to cool.
To make the glace icing, combine the icing sugar mixture and water a drop of water at a time until the mixture is smooth and it can be poured nice and thick and smooth off a spoon. There should be no lumps. It should neither be too wet and runny, or too thick and stodgy. Add the food colouring and stir until well combined.

Ice with the coloured icing mixture and then allow this to set. You can decorate the cookies any way you like, and once the icing has set, you can stack the stars from biggest first to smallest last...creating a little Christmas tree for your loved ones!

Ice Cream with Pistachio Black Salt Praline

SERVINGS: 6-8

INGREDIENTS

ICE CREAM
600ml thickened cream
1 tin condensed milk (400ml)
10ml vanilla extract

PRALINE
1 cup white sugar
1/4 cup of water
2 tablespoons pistachio
1/2 teaspoon black or white flake salt
pinch of edible petals

METHOD

Beat the cream and vanilla until stiff peaks form. Fold in the condensed milk using a metal spoon or plastic spatula. Place in a container with a lid and place in the freezer.

To make the praline, place the sugar and water in a large frying pan and boil over high heat. Shake to dissolve the sugar and allow to cook until the sugar syrup goes brown. When brown and caramel pour onto a greased baking sheet and top with the pistachios, petals and black salt flakes, allow to cool.

Break into small pieces or fine gravel when cold and then sprinkle on top of the ice cream before it sets.

Peppermint Bark

SERVINGS: 8-12

INGREDIENTS

150g/6 oz white/caramel chocolate, chopped
150g/6 oz dark/milk chocolate, chopped
1/2 cup crushed peppermint candy canes

METHOD

A classic Christmas treat made with layers of white and dark chocolate topped with crushed peppermint candies.

Place chocolate into a microwave-proof bowl. Pop in the microwave for NO MORE THAN ONE MINUTE. Stir through, there should be enough heat to melt the dark chocolate and stir until very smooth. Now spread it onto a baking/parchment-lined baking sheet.

Allow it to set in the refrigerator.
Repeat the above to melt the white chocolate. Remove the dark chocolate from the fridge and spread the melted white chocolate over the dark chocolate layer.

YOU COULD ALSO JUST USE YOUR FAVOURITE CHOCOLATE.
Sprinkle crushed candy canes on top.
Allow it to set completely, then break into pieces.
Perfect on its own, or crushed up over ice cream or panna cotta.

Christmas Hot Chocolates

SERVINGS: 2

INGREDIENTS

400 ml full cream milk
1 tablespoon cocoa powder
80g milk chocolate buttons
4 tablespoons mini marshmallows
2 candy canes for decoration

METHOD

Simply heat the milk in the microwave or in a saucepan on the stove until it boils through once.
Remove from heat and whisk in the cocoa powder and the chocolate buttons.
Stir until smooth and then serve into mugs.
Decorate with the marshmallows and the candy canes.

Gingerbread Cookies

Gingerbread Cookies

SERVINGS: 8-12

INGREDIENTS

3 cups plain, all-purpose flour
1 tsp baking powder/baking soda
1/4 tsp salt
2 heaped tablespoons of ground ginger
1 teaspoon ground cinnamon
1/2 teaspoon ground cloves
1/2 cup butter, softened
1/2 cup brown sugar
1/2 cup molasses or maple syrup
1 egg
1 set of Christmas Icing colours in tubes from the supermarket.

METHOD

In a large bowl, mix together the flour, baking soda, salt, ginger, cinnamon, and cloves.
In your stand mixer bowl, beat the butter and brown sugar until creamy, using the whisk or paddle attachment. Add molasses/maple and egg, and mix well.
Gradually add dry ingredients and mix until a dough forms.
Wrap the dough in plastic wrap and refrigerate for at least an hour.
Preheat oven to 350°F (175°C).
Roll out the dough by placing it in between two layers of plastic wrap with your rolling pin until nice and even. About 4-5mm thick. Choose a Christmassy cutter and cut out shapes. Also perfect for a gingerbread house. Place on a greased baking sheet.
Bake for about 10-12 minutes or until the edges are slightly browned.
Allow the cookies to cool before decorating with icing as desired.

CHEF'S NOTE:

They are also good just on their own. You can chop these up and use them as a ginger cookie crumble for the boozy panna cotta...they go really well together!
Why not sandwich two cookies together with a generous ice cream scoop, smash to flatten slightly, and then roll the open sides in cookie crumbs, or broken candy canes, chopped pecans, honeycomb or chocolate curls.

Sticky Date & Brandy Pudding

Sticky Date & Brandy Pudding

SERVINGS: 8-12

INGREDIENTS

250g stoned dates, chopped soaked in 250ml hot water
3ml bicarbonate of soda
140g butter
400g white sugar (200g for cake and 200g for sauce)
2 large eggs
250g flour
2 teaspoons baking powder
2ml salt
100g pecan nuts, chopped
125ml brandy
200ml water

METHOD

Pre-heat your oven to 180°C and grease a 2L (8 cup) baking dish.
Soak the dates in 250 ml hot water and mix well. Beat the butter and 200g of the sugar together until light and fluffy, now add the eggs and beat. Stir in the sifted flour and salt. Add the dates and nuts and mix until well combined. Spoon into a greased baking dish.

Make the syrup by mixing the remaining 200g sugar with the 125 ml brandy and 200 ml water & pour gently over the cake mixture using the back of a spoon.
NOTE: Make sure the mixture only reaches halfway up the side of your baking dish or else the sauce will boil over and ruin your oven! Bake for about 25-30 minutes in an oven of 180C until done.

Serve hot with custard, whipped cream, or ice cream! It's decadently simple and everyone's favourite. It can be baked in individual ramekins at a reduced cooking time of about 8 – 10 minutes!

Christmas Trifle Cups

SERVINGS: 8

INGREDIENTS

450 g Chocolate cake or vanilla sponge cake cubed
1 litre Custard or vanilla pudding
1 x 300 ml batch of strawberry or cherry jelly, diced
500g Mixed berries (strawberries, blueberries, raspberries)
600 ml cream, Whipped lightly seasoned with 10ml vanilla and 1 g nutmeg
Optional: 80-100ml sherry or other liquor for soaking the cake
8 Sprigs of Christmassy herbs like rosemary
8 Cinnamon Quills and Star Anise stars for decoration
8 Dried orange slices for garnish

METHOD

Layer cubed cake at the bottom of a trifle dish or glass.
Drizzle with liquor and/or jelly liquid or cubes if the jelly is pre-made.
Add a layer of custard or vanilla pudding over the cake.
Add a layer of mixed berries.
Repeat the layers until the dish is filled, finishing with a layer of whipped cream and some berries for decoration.
Refrigerate for a few hours before serving.
Remember to adjust these recipes according to your preferences and dietary restrictions.
Enjoy making these delicious Christmas desserts!

Make as many as you need. I would allow 4 tablespoons of cake, jelly and custard per cup.
These are great because you can make them and store them for up to three days in the fridge.
Simply pipe the cream and decorate just before you serve.

NOTES

NOTES

This book is It is about taking your festive leftovers and transforming them into delicious, colourful and exciting dishes.

THE LITTLE BOOK OF
Christmas Leftovers

With Chef Mel Alafaci

Leftover Inspiration Cookbook

Leftovers are my favourite thing. I love having some versatile and reliable recipes and ideas to help use up precious and delicious Christmas fare for many days after the big day.

A great tip I learned from my fantastic mother-in-law was to store the ham in the fridge in a clean pillowcase soaked in white vinegar, for storing the ham safely in the fridge for days to come.
What a spectacular idea, and one I am proud to share with you.

This book is filled with some of my ideas on how to use up those Christmas leftovers.

Leftovers make you feel good twice!

Recipes

52	Glamorous Turkey & Cream Cheese Balls
53	Crispy Spring Rolls
54	Croquettes
55	Stuffed Chicken
56	Party Pies
58	The Ultimate Leftover Stacks
59	Quesadillas
60	Chef's Salad with Mel's Secret Dressing
62	Happy Sexy Quickie Eggs
63	Tea Cup Quiche

Glamorous Turkey & Cream Cheese Balls

SERVINGS: 6-8

INGREDIENTS

125 g cream cheese softened
250-500 g chicken or turkey meat cooked and shredded
Zest of one lemon
1 cup chopped broccoli, fennel, cauliflower, green bean, capsicum, cabbage, celery, kale etc.
1 teaspoon mustard
1 cup freshly chopped parsley, chives or similar

METHOD

Simply mix the cooked cooled chicken or turkey with the cream cheese, zest, pepper, mustard, and veggies.

Stir to bind and then roll into balls.

Drop each ball into and through the chopped parsley and chives and ready to serve on a starter platter, snack, or quick easy dinner!

NOTE: these can then be served with crackers or toasted sourdough. Delicious.

Crispy Spring Rolls

SERVINGS: 6-8

INGREDIENTS

2 cups shredded or diced leftover turkey and veggies, use your favourite mix here
1 teaspoon grated ginger
3-4 chopped spring onions, green bits included
12-16 sheets of spring roll pastry, from the freezer aisle of your local supermarket. *Defrost before use*
1 egg beaten with 100 ml water to make an egg wash to seal the spring rolls
2 tablespoons vegetable oil or melted butter to brush the shaped spring rolls

METHOD

Ensure your filling is cold, stir in the ginger and the spring onions. You can simply chop or dice or blend your delicious leftovers to form a delightful spring roll filling.

Unwrap the spring roll sheet and place one in front of you, with one of the corners facing toward you. Brush the opposite corners with some of the egg wash, then place a large tablespoon of the filling on the corner closest to you. There should be rolling diagrams on the spring roll packaging.
Now roll up away from you to securely wrap the filling in securely. Fold the left and right in over the filling and then continue to roll forward to complete the spring roll parcel.

Brush with the melted butter or vegetable oil and set aside.
Continue until you have used all the filling and the sheets, brush all of them with the oil or the butter, and then bake in a preheated oven of 200c for 12-15 minutes until gorgeous and brown OR pop in the air fryer for 8-12 minutes until brown and crunchy.

Serve with sweet chilli sauce or your favourite dipping sauce. Enjoy!

Croquettes

SERVINGS: 6-8

INGREDIENTS

2 cups cold potato mash
or mashed-up leftover roast vegetables like potatoes, carrots, sweet potatoes etc.
1 cup chopped or diced cooked but cold turkey or ham
1 cup breadcrumbs (half for the filling and half to coat the croquette)
1 egg
100g grated cheddar cheese
2 tablespoons freshly chopped parsley or spring onion

METHOD

Croquettes are actually a typical French dish, but they are currently popular in Spain, Sicily, and the Netherlands. Making your own croquettes are so very easy and hiding valuable Christmas leftovers into gloriously crunchy morsels is practically genius.

In a large mixing bowl mix the mashed vegetables, diced or chopped leftover turkey or ham, the egg, and half a cup of breadcrumbs, and the freshly chopped parsley or spring onion. You should have a dry mash. Season to taste with salt and pepper. Please make sure this mixture is nice and dry, if it is a bit wet, add another half a cup of breadcrumbs and that should firm the mixture up.

Place the other half of the cup of breadcrumbs in a wide bowl. Take a tablespoonful of the mixture and place it in the breadcrumbs. Shake to coat the spoonful in the crumbs so it is easy to handle when you grab it out and then form it into a cylinder shape or just a lazy ball. The crumbs should stick easily to the wet mix. Set aside on a plate or board and continue until it is all processed. You may need to top up the breadcrumbs if you run out.

Spray with some cooking oil or melted butter to wet and coat the breadcrumbs, and then either bake on a greased tray in a hot oven of 200c for 12-15 minutes until nice and browned or cook them in your air fryer for 12-15 minutes in batches until nice and crunchy.

You can also deep fry or shallow fry these in hot oil if you prefer.

Perfect snacks or starters to serve with a dipping sauce of your choice.

Stuffed Chicken

SERVINGS: 6

INGREDIENTS

1 large chicken	**SWEET POTATO & HAM STUFFING**
1 quantity Sweet Potato and Ham stuffing	2 cups roasted sweet potato
	1 cup diced leftover ham or bacon
SPRAY TAN	2 small onions, chopped
1 teaspoon turmeric powder	2 cloves garlic
1 teaspoon ras el hanout OR curry powder	50-100g feta, goats cheese or ricotta
30ml Oil	1 teaspoon sage, chopped
Salt & Pepper	

METHOD

To make the stuffing start by browning the ham in a bit of oil in a hot pan, not stirring too much, but allowing it to brown off nicely. Add the onion and garlic and cook through. Remove from heat and add the cooked mashed sweet potato, cheese, and sage. Mix to combine, season, and set aside.

Cut chicken down the back –just to the side of the backbone. Place chicken skin side up on a chopping board, head and neck side closest to you. Now start loosening the skin off the breast meat and work all the way under the skin, reduce the skin on the thighs and legs of the chicken make an envelope, and use a spoon to stuff the bird under the skin with the stuffing.

Spray tan or brush the chicken with turmeric mixed with some oil. Roast in a hot oven (200°C) for about 35 minutes until cooked.

TO SERVE

Cut each chicken in half and serve with cauliflower puree and steamed green beans and zucchini in a lemony buttery sauce, topped with pistachio crumbs, black salt, petals, and micro-herbs.

Party Pies

SERVINGS: 6-8

INGREDIENTS

4 sheets of puff pastry
1 egg beaten with 100 ml milk to make an egg wash
2 cups leftovers chopped up to form a lovely, tasty filling, must be cold.
1 teaspoon poppy or sesame seeds or grated parmesan cheese, optional.

METHOD

Place two sheets of the puff pastry on a large enough greased baking tray. Brush egg wash on the borders of both pieces of pastry. Pack the filling from the middle of the pastry, but keep the edges or the borders of the pastry with the egg wash clean and free of filling.

Dust the remaining two pieces of puff pastry with a little flour.
Fold the first piece in half and use a sharp paring knife to cut through the fold of the pastry nicely and sharply and neatly, but leave the borders intact. This is referred to as a lattice cut.

Open this latticed lid and place it over one of the filled pieces on the baking tray. Press down to seal the edges or use a fork to press this down. Do the same with the second piece and then brush both latticed lids with some of the remaining egg wash. Garnish with poppy or sesame seeds. You can either bake, refrigerate or even freeze these party pies to cook at a later stage. They can be stored in the fridge like this for up to two days, or with a stable filling in the freezer for about 3 months. You can cook it from frozen! Never freeze raw mushrooms or tomatoes in your filling.

Now pre-heat the oven to 200c and place into the fridge first for at least 20 minutes to allow the handled pastry to cool.

Once the oven is at temperature, bake for 15-18 minutes until golden brown.
Serve and enjoy.

The Ultimate Leftover Stacks

57

The Ultimate Leftover Stacks

SERVINGS: 6-8

INGREDIENTS

200g leftover shredded turkey or ham or other
50ml - 100ml fat-free yogurt or a nice thick real mayonnaise
1 tablespoon freshly chopped mint and/or basil
1 granny smith apple, cored and finely sliced
Half a cup of finely sliced red cabbage, fennel, lettuce, or anything you have that is crunchy
1 cup finely chopped broccoli: I use my knife and make this into rice
Lots of ground black pepper
1 teaspoon grainy mustard
1 English cucumber, make into ribbons using your peeler (or slightly roast zucchini ribbons instead)
Slices of roasted sweet potato, lightly coated in your favourite spice:
be creative and use your leftover vegetables
1 sweet potato cut into ribbons with a peeler or julienne peeler to get them like mine/;
roasted with a bit of oil and seasoning in the oven *or air fryer and then allow to cool*

METHOD

Leave the cucumber ribbons until the end, you can make them and keep them in the fridge until ready to assemble if you like.
Mix the rest of the ingredients together as if you are making a coleslaw; the mayonnaise or yogurt will bind all the ingredients together.
Season to taste.

Now assemble it as a stack by doing the following.
Place one large tablespoon of the filling on the centre of the plate.
Grab a cucumber ribbon and wrap it around this filling to form a neat bundle, the cucumber ribbon will stick to itself, allowing you to wrap around the filling and make a high cylinder.
Now, fill the cucumber ribbon cylinder with more of the filling.
You can make these as big or as small as you like.

Quesadillas

SERVINGS: 1

INGREDIENTS

1 large tortilla wrap
½ cup Sliced ham or turkey
½ cup Leftover veggies of your choice
50g Sliced or grated cheese
20 g Chipotle sauce or mayo

METHOD

Using a folded-over tortilla wrap is pure genius for using up valuable leftovers.

Place the sliced ham or turkey over half the tortilla wrap and top with the diced or sliced cheese. Season with your choice of sauce.

Fold the other side of the tortilla over this and then cook in a sandwich press for about 2-3 minutes until the tortilla is deliciously toasted and the cheese has melted.

Remove and eat.

You can use two tortillas for this and then make the filling spread all over the base and then top with the second one. This will make you a larger one so whatever suits the family.

Chef's Salad with Mel's Secret Dressing

SERVINGS: 1

INGREDIENTS

1 large handful rocket or assorted salad leaves into the bottom of the bowl
Handful grated cheddar cheese
4-5 halved cherry tomatoes
6 cucumber slices, optional
1 tablespoon olives, optional
¼ sliced capsicum/peppers
¼ cut shaved red cabbage OR sliced red onions
¼ cup sliced turkey or ham or chicken

DRESSING

1 heaped tablespoon of good mayonnaise
Large pinch of cracked black pepper
Pinch of freshly grated lemon zest, optional
20-30 ml cold tap water

METHOD

This is my favourite salad to make for the family, and it allows me to use what is in the fridge and needs to be used up. You will LOVE this sexy and easy dressing. It is super simple, and I use it for almost every salad I make.
I make these into individual salad bowls so no one has to share.
This is for one bowl, make as many as you need.

Simply place these ingredients in a cup or small bowl and mix the mayo with the water until it makes a smooth paste, then this can be used to drizzle over your sexy salads.

Happy Sexy Quickie Eggs

Happy Sexy Quickie Eggs

SERVINGS: 2

INGREDIENTS

Vegetable oil or cooking spray (not olive oil)
2 tablespoons chopped/diced bacon (leftovers are perfect)
OR Prosciutto/Pancetta OR Speck OR chorizo sausage OR mushrooms *(you choose)*
2 tablespoons chopped onions
OR Spinach OR spring onion OR zucchini OR tomato OR leftover veggies
3-4 fresh free-range eggs
1 pinch of pepper to season
1 tablespoon grated cheddar
Pecorino or Parmesan (optional)
Drizzle of truffle oil, and extra virgin olive oil (optional)

METHOD

In my quest for the laziest YET sexiest eggs, this has become one of my best inventions.
It's almost a cross between an omelette and a fried egg - but the best of both!
Omelettes have the privilege of having a filling to make them a bit sexier.
Fried eggs are okay, but the large expanse of tasteless egg white is just not my favourite.
With this recipe, the white will be loaded with amazing flavour, colour and texture and will look ten bucks more expensive. Also, unless you have a fabulous pan, omelettes can make your language very bad when they stick and break and just don't turn out. Literally.
So, try my happy eggs, you can change the 'filling' to whatever you like.
I'll give you a few ideas and let you have a happy egg all by yourself! Enjoy.

You will need a small to medium frying pan with a lid for this recipe.
Heat and grease the frying pan well with the cooking spray. You DO NOT want to underdo the oiling and risk all your ingredients sticking. Place the diced bacon *(or speck, chorizo or mushrooms)* in the pan and let them go crisp and brown and flavoursome. Add the second ingredient *(onion, spring onion or zucchini)* and cook while stirring for about a minute until soft.
Now spread it evenly around the pan.
Crack the eggs over this deliciousness and then turn the heat to medium, put the lid on the pan and let those eggs cook through to the doneness you like: soft, medium or hard.
Season with pepper oil, and it's ready to serve!

Tea Cup Quiche

SERVINGS: 1

INGREDIENTS

1 teacup (most of them are ovenproof) or pie shell lightly greased with cooking spray or butter
1 slice of bread buttered, crust removed
1 egg beaten
1 teaspoon grated cheddar cheese
Pinch salt and pepper
1-2 tablespoons chopped ham or turkey (leftovers are perfect here)
Fresh herbs or leaves like basil or rocket to garnish when cooked

METHOD

I love this recipe, it really is so easy but it is one you need to know.
This recipe is for one individual portion, but of course, make as many as you like.

Place the buttered bread butter side down into the ovenproof teacup or pie dish or tart tin and press down the thin out and shape the piece of bread. This is a clever trick instead of having to make a pastry.

Add the beaten egg, seasoning and filling, and cheese and bake in the oven at 180-200c for about 12-15 minutes until the bread is nice and brown and the egg is cooked. This will depend on the depth of your teacup or pie dish, the deeper it is the longer it will take.

I used my air fryer once or twice; was amazing! Took about 8 minutes on the frozen chip setting.

NOTES

Meet Chef Mel
THE HAPPY CHEF

PASSIONATE FOODIE, AUTHOR, ENTREPRENEUR, COOKING SCHOOL TEACHER, ATHLETE, CULTURAL GASTRONOMER AND CHEF

With a smile that can light up a room she has been dubbed "The Happy Chef" by her students, Chef Mel is brilliant at making everyday dishes dazzling. Her clever approach to cooking and teaching focuses on making recipes easy to understand, with time spent on excellent presentation skills.

The enthusiastic, entertaining, award-winning African-Australian chef and cooking school owner says that with a bit of know-how, anyone can plate up spectacular spreads like those you would expect to see in five-star restaurants. Her intoxicating enthusiasm, authenticity and culinary lingo will have you hungry to flex your muscles in the kitchen.

She promises that this book will teach you some seriously cheffy skills so that you will be so much more confident and happy in your kitchen.

She can't wait to help you become the foodie you have always wanted to be!

Get ready to make delicious discoveries!

www.ingramcontent.com/pod-product-compliance
Lightning Source LLC
Chambersburg PA
CBHW061802290426
44109CB00030B/2924